Science Matters
ROCKS

Melanie Ostopowich

WEIGL PUBLISHERS INC.

Published by Weigl Publishers Inc.
350 5th Avenue, Suite 3304, PMB 6G
New York, NY USA 10118-0069
Web site: www.weigl.com

Library of Congress Cataloging-in-Publication Data

Ostopowich, Melanie.
  Rocks / Melanie Ostopowich.
      p. cm. -- (Science matters)
  Includes index.
  ISBN 1-59036-210-1 (lib. bdg. : alk. paper) ISBN 1-59036-252-7 (softcover)
1. Rocks--Juvenile literature. 2. Petrology--Juvenile literature. I. Title. II. Series.
  QE432.2.O88 2005
  552--dc22

                              2004004135

Printed in the United States of America
1 2 3 4 5 6 7 8 9 0 08 07 06 05 04

Project Coordinator Tina Schwartzenberger **Copy Editor** Heather Kissock
Design Terry Paulhus **Layout** Bryan Pezzi
Photo Researcher Ellen Bryan

Photograph Credits

Every reasonable effort has been made to trace ownership and to obtain permission to reprint copyright material. The publishers would be pleased to have any errors or omissions brought to their attention so that they may be corrected in subsequent printings.

Cover: Canyonlands National Park, Utah from Photos.com
COMSTOCK: page 8; **Corel Corporation:** page 6; **David Liebman:** page 17; **NASA:** page 19 (Eugene Cernan); **Bryan Pezzi:** pages 7, 12-13; **PhotoDisc:** page 16; **Photos.com:** pages 1, 3T, 3M, 3B, 4, 6, 7, 10, 11, 14, 18, 21, 22T, 22B, 23T, 23B; **Roger Weller:** pages 9,15.

Contents

Studying Rocks

Rocks are everywhere. They lie by the sides of roads and in backyards. They form Earth's **crust**. Rocks are found at the bottoms of rivers and lakes. They are also found on mountain peaks. Sand, dust, boulders, and mountains are all rocks.

The study of Earth's **structure** is called geology. Geologists are scientists who study rocks, mountains, and cliffs to learn what Earth is made from. They also learn how Earth has changed over time.

● Canyons are formed by rivers cutting through rock. Layers of rock can be seen in the canyon walls.

Rock Facts

Although rocks are not alive, they are changing all the time. Read on to learn more interesting facts about rocks.

- The oldest known rock was found in Canada. It is nearly 4 billion years old.

- Rocks are made of two or more **minerals**.

- There are hundreds of rock types. Only 20 common types of rocks are found on Earth's surface.

- Up to 100,000 tons (90,718 tonnes) of rock fall to Earth from space each year.

- Sometimes lightning strikes sand on a beach. The heat melts the tiny rocks that make up the sand to form a glassy rock called fulgurite.

Types of Rock

Geologists group rocks into three main types. These groups are based on how rocks form. Igneous rocks are made when **lava** cools. Sedimentary rocks are formed when layers of **sediment** become stuck together. Heat and pressure cause sedimentary and igneous rocks to change. A new type of rock, called metamorphic rock, forms.

■ Sedimentary rock is fragile. It is easily broken down by wind and rain.

Rock Words

Rocks can be called by many names. The word used often tells the size of the rock. Here are some rock words. Can you think of any others?

PEBBLE: a small rock, usually rounded, that can be held with two fingers

STONE: a medium-sized rock that can be held in two hands

BOULDER: a large rock that is taller than a person

RIVER ROCK: round rocks found along the edges and at the bottom of fast-flowing rivers

MOUNTAIN: a giant piece of rock that is attached to Earth's crust and does not move

Earth Rocks

The planet Earth is one big rock. Earth's core is made of molten, or melted, rock. The crust is made of rocks and minerals. Ice, water, **soil**, and sand cover much of the crust.

Rocks on Earth can be changed in two ways. Weathering is the breaking down of rocks on Earth's surface by natural forces such as frost, rain, and heat. Erosion is the removal of rock and pieces of soil by natural forces such as running water, ice, waves, and wind. These processes are part of the rock cycle.

● Earth's solid crust is rock. Beneath the surface is molten, or melted, rock called magma.

Space Rocks

The Moon is a big rock, too. Like Earth, it is made up of smaller rocks. Scientists have brought rocks from the Moon to Earth for study.

Scientists have found that rocks from the Moon are made of the same materials as some rocks on Earth. The Moon's surface is mostly made of **basalt**. Basalt is the most common type of rock on Earth's surface. Most of the ocean floor is also basalt. Moon basalt is darker in color and more **dense** than Earth basalt.

Sometimes rocks fall to Earth from space. These rocks are called meteorites when they are on Earth.

Rocks and Minerals

All the rocks, pebbles, and sand on Earth are made from minerals. Minerals are solid materials that are found in the natural environment. They are made of materials that were never alive.

About 3,000 different kinds of minerals have been found on Earth. All rocks are made from at least two kinds of minerals.

■ The Garden of the Gods Park in Colorado Springs, Colorado, is famous for sandstone rock formations. Sandstone contains the minerals quartz and feldspar.

Sparkle

Some rocks are dull. Others are colorful. Some rocks reflect light. These rocks sparkle.

Crystals are solid substances. The pieces that make up crystals are arranged in regular patterns. Most crystals reflect light very well, so they appear to sparkle. If rocks sparkle, it is usually because they have crystal inside.

Crystal is not the only reason rocks sparkle. Rocks are made from minerals. Some minerals are metallic. These minerals contain metal. Metal is shiny and reflects light. Some rocks that sparkle have metallic minerals inside them.

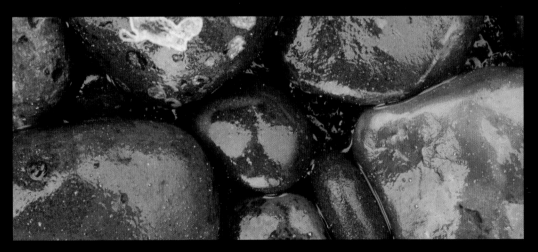

● When rocks are wet, dirt and sand are washed away. The minerals in the rocks sparkle and shine.

The Rock Cycle

The process in which rocks form, break down, and reform is called the rock cycle. It takes thousands of years for one rock to change.

Over time, all types of rocks break apart and become sediments. Wind and rain cause sediments to gather and pile up. Pressure from gathering sediment creates sedimentary rock.

High temperature and pressure can change sedimentary and igneous rocks into metamorphic rocks. New igneous rocks form from cooled lava.

Sedimentary Rocks

Metamorphic Rocks

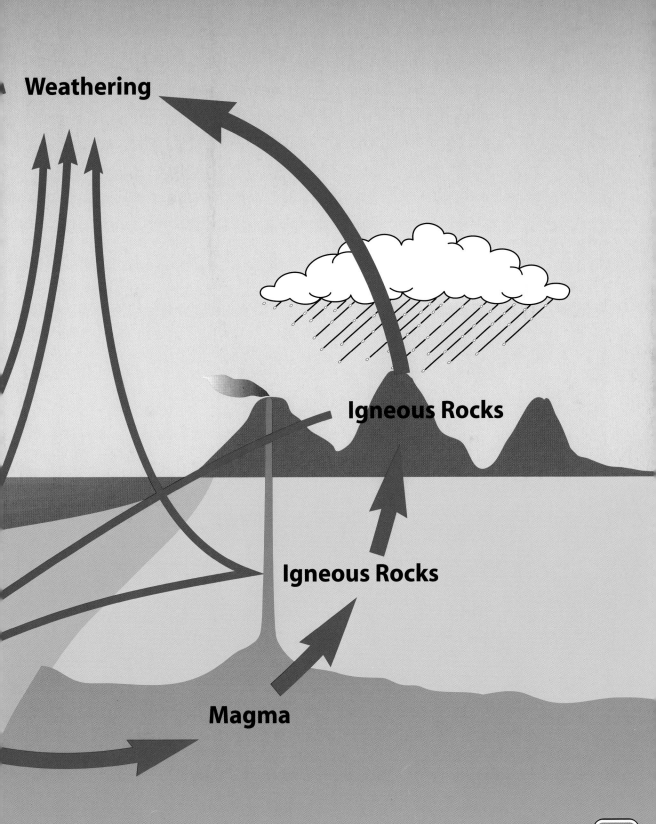

Weathering

Igneous Rocks

Igneous Rocks

Magma

13

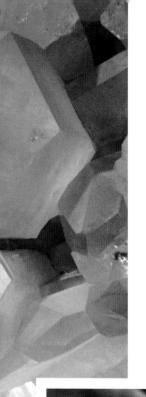

Gemstones

A gemstone is a rock or mineral used for jewelry or decoration. Some gemstones are very expensive. Their value depends on their beauty, how common they are, and their **hardness**. Gemstones that can be cut to reflect their luster, or shine, are the most valuable. Less than 100 minerals are used as gemstones. The most valuable gemstones are diamonds, rubies, and emeralds.

● When diamonds are cut and polished for gemstones, about half of the original diamond is lost.

Geodes

A geode looks like a plain, ordinary rock. However, the inside is hollow and filled with crystals.

A geode develops from either sedimentary rock or volcanic rock. Volcanic rock is igneous rock that forms from cooled magma. In volcanic rock, geodes begin forming when a bubble forms in hardening lava.

In sedimentary rock, a geode begins as a hollow area inside the sediments. As the rock forms, a hard shell surrounds the bubble or hollow area. Water containing dissolved minerals gets inside the rock. As the water evaporates, minerals remain inside the rock. Over time, the minerals inside the rock harden and become crystals.

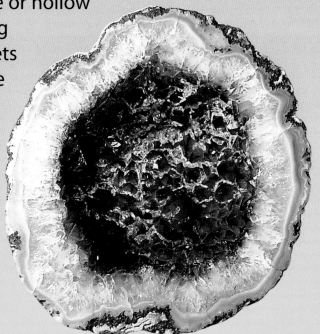

Rock Uses

Rocks have many uses. Rocks are used to make roads, buildings, and sidewalks. Many cities today are built with stones. A building has a foundation, which is the base that the building sits on. Foundations are often made with rocks.

The average North American uses more than 1,000,000 pounds (453,592 kilograms) of stone, sand, gravel, and cement in his or her lifetime. These rock materials are used as concrete in buildings and as crushed stone in roads. Rocks are also used for decoration.

● Rocks are a popular addition to gardens and pathways. They help keep moisture in the soil.

Become a Rock Hound

Someone who collects rocks is called a rock hound. Would you like to become a rock hound?

Start your collection by picking up rocks. Collect rocks you find in your yard, on your way to school, and in the schoolyard. Cliffs, hills, **quarries**, and roadsides are also good places to look for rocks. You can store your rock collection in a shoe box or egg carton.

Label where you found each rock and when you collected it. Try to identify each type of rock in your collection. Do you think it is igneous, metamorphic, or sedimentary? You may need to visit the library or search the Internet to learn what types of rocks you have found.

Fossils in Rocks

A fossil is the rocklike remains of a plant or animal. Fossils are usually found in sedimentary rock. Plants or animals that have died get trapped among layers of sediment. After a long time, these layers of sediment turn into sedimentary rock. The animal or plant remains are preserved, or protected, inside the rock. Fossils tell scientists what life was like on Earth long ago.

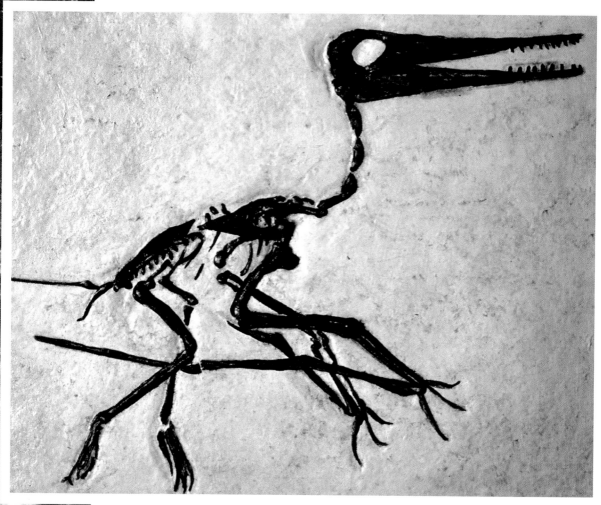

● Fossils of dinosaurs such as the pterodactyl are found in rocks. Fossils teach scientists about animals in Earth's past.

A Life of Science

Harrison (Jack) Schmitt

Harrison (Jack) Schmitt helped train astronauts flying to the Moon. Schmitt taught the astronauts how to be geologists when they were on the Moon. He taught the astronauts what kind of rocks to look for and bring back to Earth.

In 1972, Schmitt flew to the Moon on *Apollo 17*. This was the last human flight to the Moon. On the Moon, Schmitt and his fellow astronauts spent hours collecting rock samples. They brought 243 pounds (110 kg) of rock samples back to Earth—the most ever gathered. Schmitt studied these rocks to learn more about the Moon.

Surfing Our Earth

How can I find more information about rocks?

- Libraries have many interesting books about rocks.
- Science centers and museums are great places to learn about rocks.
- The Internet offers some great Web sites dedicated to rocks.

Where can I find a good reference Web site to learn more about rocks?

Encarta Homepage

www.encarta.com

- Type any rock-related term into the search engine. Some terms to try include "mineral" and "geology."

How can I find out more about rocks, the rock cycle, and fossils?

Windows to the Universe

www.windows.ucar.edu

- Click on "Geology" to learn about the three types of rock, scientists who study rocks, and fossils.

Science in Action

Grow Your Own Crystals

Most crystals take thousands of years to grow. However, salt crystals grow very quickly. You can grow them yourself.

You will need:

- a glass jar
- a pencil
- a piece of thread
- salt

Fill the jar half full with warm water. Stir salt in the water until no more salt will dissolve. Attach the thread to the pencil. Rest the pencil across the top of the jar so the thread hangs into the water. Do not let the thread touch the bottom of the jar. As the water evaporates, salt crystals will form on the thread. Use a magnifying glass to look at the crystals. Can you see the crystal cubes?

What Have You Learned?

1 How old is the oldest rock that has been found?

2 How much rock falls to Earth each year from space?

3 What are rocks that fall to Earth from space called?

4 What are rocks made from?

5 What kind of rock forms from lava?

6 What is a rock used for jewelry called?

7 What type of rock is hollow with crystals inside?

8 What is a fossil?

9 Why did geologist Harrison Schmitt go to the Moon?

10 How many common types of rocks are found on Earth?

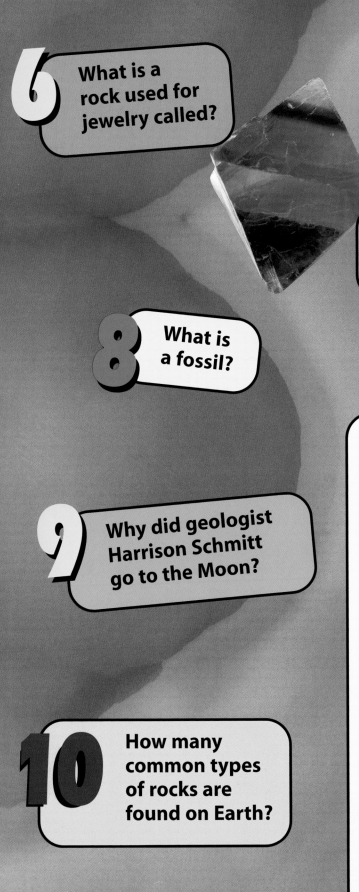

Answers: 1. The oldest rock found was nearly 4 billion years old. **2.** 100,000 tons (90,718 t) **3.** Meteorites **4.** Rocks are made from two or more minerals. **5.** Igneous rock **6.** A gemstone **7.** A geode **8.** A fossil is the rocklike remains of a plant or animal. **9.** He went to collect rocks to study to learn about the Moon. **10.** 20

Words to Know

basalt: a hard rock formed in very hot conditions

crust: Earth's hard, top layer

crystals: solid substances with flat surfaces and regular shape

dense: crowded close together

hardness: ability of a substance to resist being scratched

lava: melted rock that comes out of an erupting volcano

minerals: solid materials in the natural environment that were never alive

quarries: places where stone is dug, cut, or blasted for use in building

sediment: very small pieces of rock and dirt deposited by water, wind, or ice

soil: tiny pieces of rock that form the top layer of the ground in which plants grow

structure: the way the parts that make something are arranged

Index